There's a 'U' and an 'I' in unity
costs the earth and yet it's free.

My grandad's from Tuvalu and to be specific
it's plop bang in the middle of the South Pacific

the smallest of our 53 Commonwealth nations
the largest in terms of reading vast constellations

my ancestors were guided by sky and sea trails
and way before Columbus even hoisted his sails!

What we leave behind matters to those who go before
we face the future with our backs, sailing shore to shore

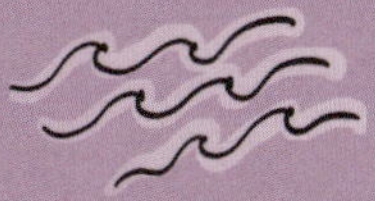

for we're earning and saving for our common wealth
a common strong body, a common good health

for the salt in the sea, like the salt in our blood
like the dust of our bones, our final return to mud

means saving the ocean, saving the bee
means London in the UK seeing Ronton in the South Seas
and sharing our thoughts over a cuppa tea

for there's a 'U' and an 'I' in unity
costs the earth and yet it's free.

MOPHEAD TU

* Tu: to stand with integrity

That's when your insides match your outsides.

MOPHEAD TU*
The Queen's Poem

by Selina Tusitala Marsh

She drew me again!

AUCKLAND
UNIVERSITY
PRESS

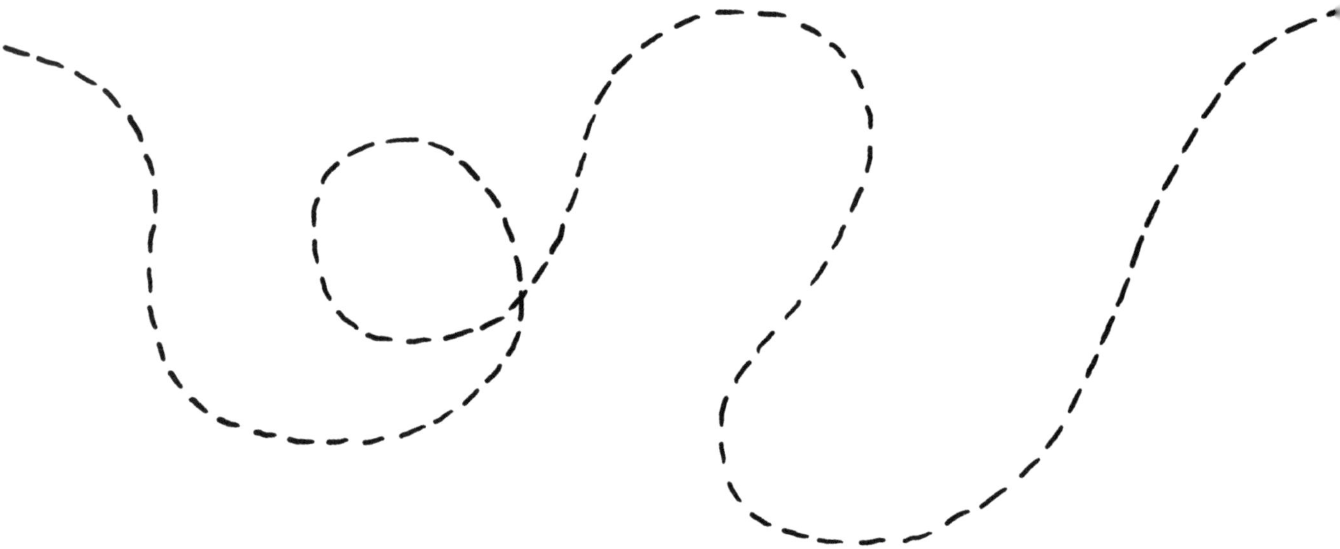

One day, I received
a letter from the
Queen of England.

I wonder if it's because we share the same birthday, 21st April!
EIIR
FAST TALKING PI

I'd been crowned the

Your service to the Queen:
Write her a poem.
FINE PRINT
What's the Commonwealth?

The Commonwealth
is made up of countries
the Queen used to rule.
They were called

colonies.

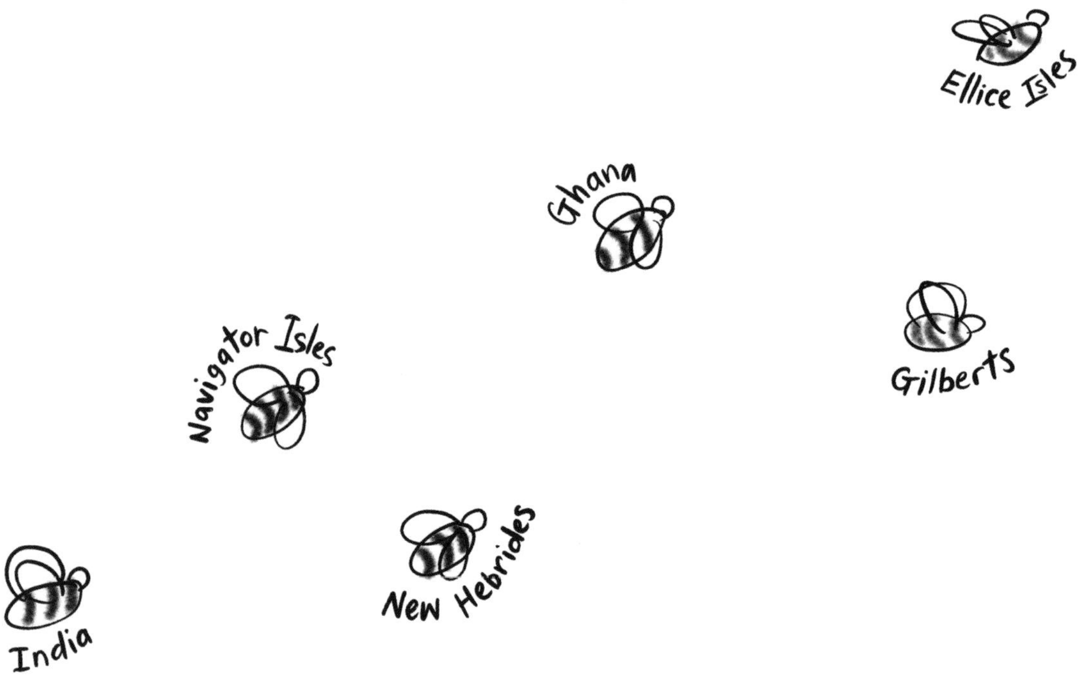

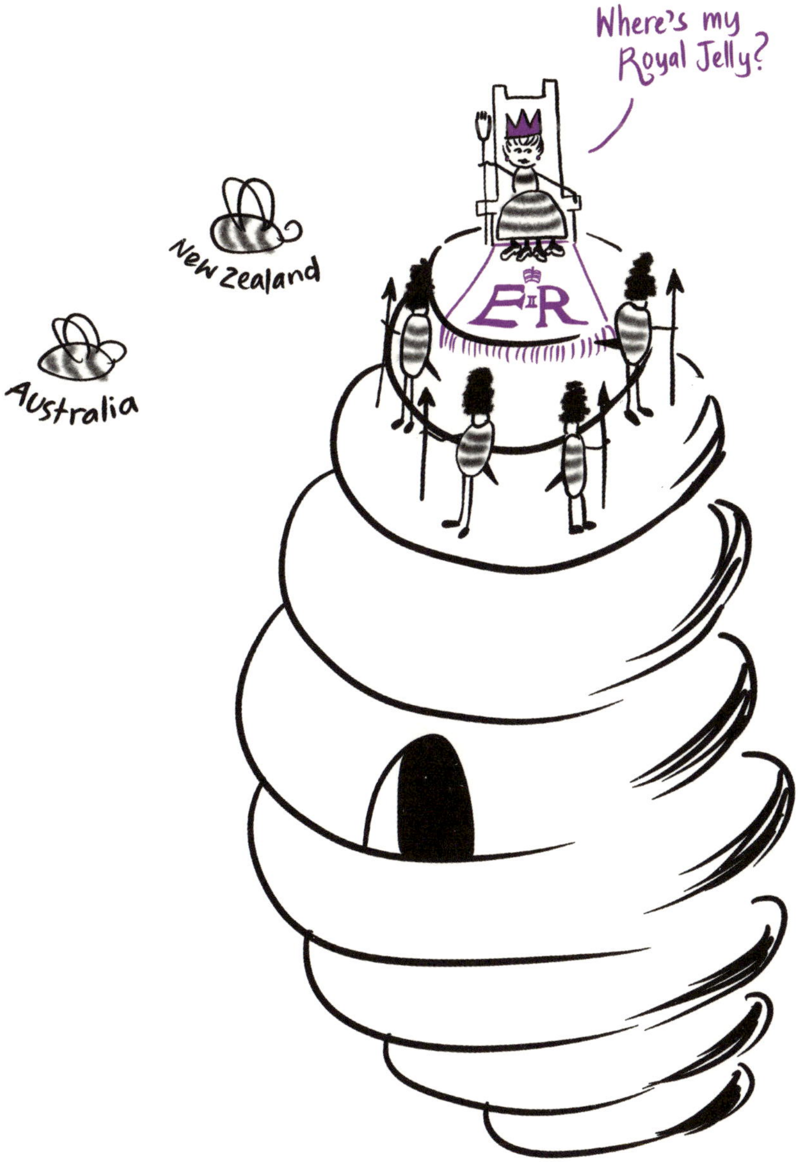

The Queen's hive was

strong and powerful.

She got to make all the rules
for her colonies.

She could name them,

claim them,
Captain Cook, DISCOVERER of the Pacific
COLUMBUS
Who's that dude pointing at the stars?
That's Tupaia, Cook's navigator. But school doesn't teach that story.

shame them
GOD
gods
That's not right.

and tame them.
We bring order and peace...
...and boxes to take and sell your stuff in.
PHOSPHATE
mineral
SUGAR
COCONUTS
Spice
GUANO
bird poop!

But no one likes to be bullied.

That's called COLONIALISM.

So the colonies started breaking the

Queen's

rules

and making their own.

Talofa! I'm Tusitala, Mophead's grandad.
This is Piglet, my piglet.
ELLICE
TUVALU

Ending colonial rule
wasn't easy.

MAU
TAMASESE
SAMOA MO S
COLON LISI
GET UP
STAND UP
FOR YOUR
RIGHTS!
OUR ISland
OUR RULES

People died.
Many are still struggling.

MAU MAU
THE LAND AND FREEDOM MOVEMENT
DECOLONISE NOW!
MARCH FOR FREEDOM!!
TRICK or TREATY?
KIA MAU

... So when I got my crown, not
all my friends were happy about it.

SELLOUT*
That's when your insides **DON'T** match your outsides.

Can I stand up for my people who struggled against the Queen...
...and still serve the Queen?

I got out my journal.

Where do
I
stand?
Selina Tusitala Marsh

The answers were
inside me.

TUSI

TALA

— I'm in the middle!

I've always stood in the middle.

I grew up being caught in the middle,

stuck in the middle,

and felt like I had to choose sides.

RCE

But I wouldn't choose one side,
not at home.

I want to be with you both.
Mum
Dad

Not at school.

Not on the street.

Are you Samoan?
Are you English?
Are you French?
Are you Tuvaluan?
Are you Scottish?

Yes!
AFAKASI

Not at university.

Are you a Pacific Island poet?
Or a Pacific Island scholar?
Yes!
I am a Pasifika poet-scholar

But why do I stand in the middle?
Tusitala
ala = bridge

Again, the answers were
inside me.

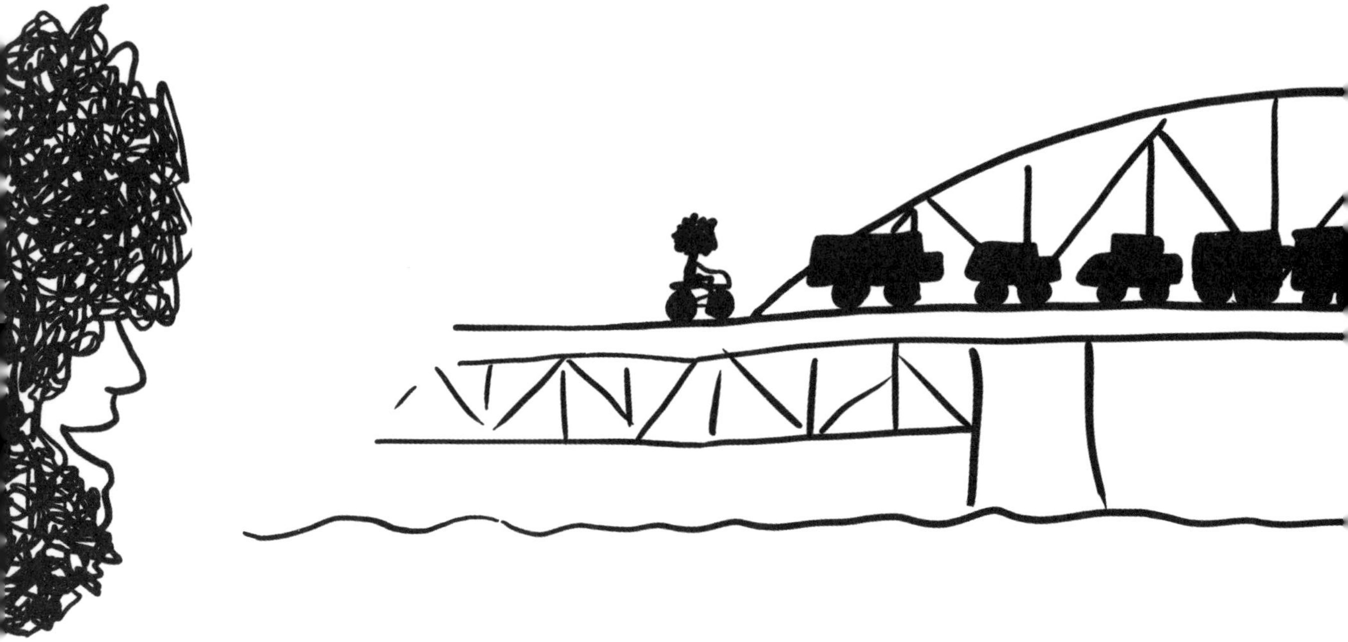

I bridge,

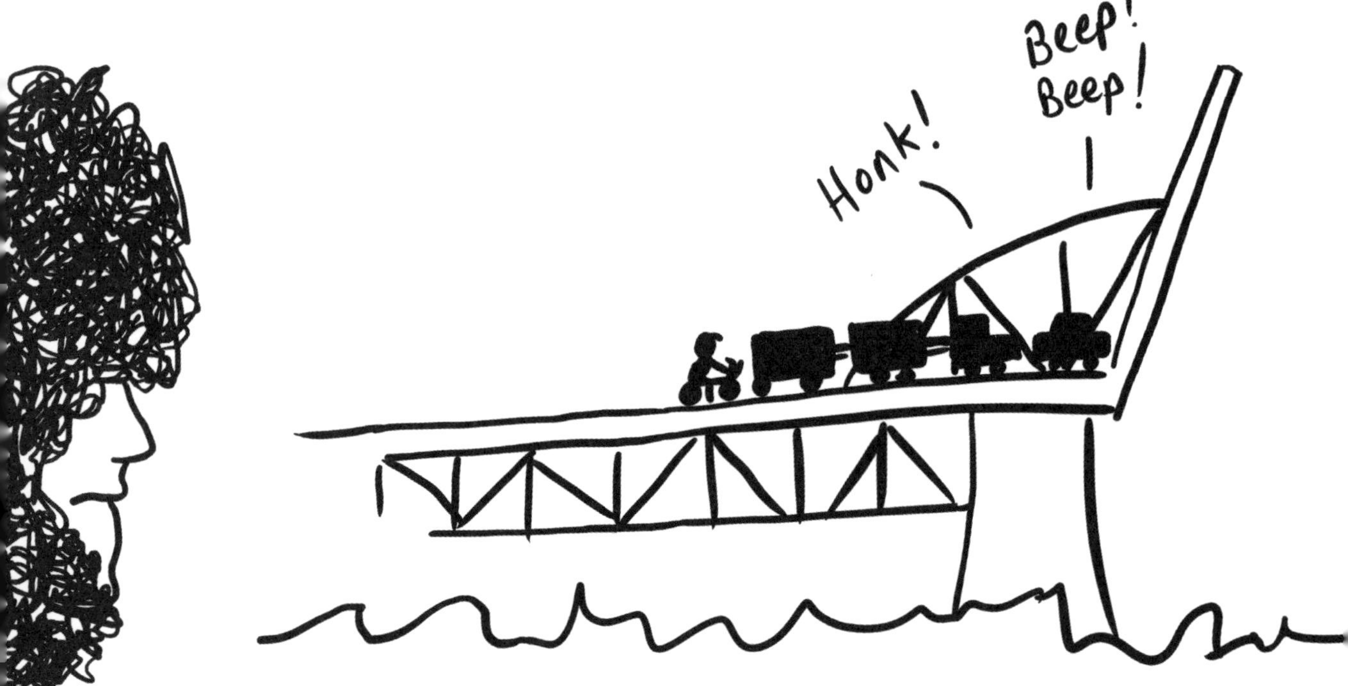
Honk!
Beep! Beep!

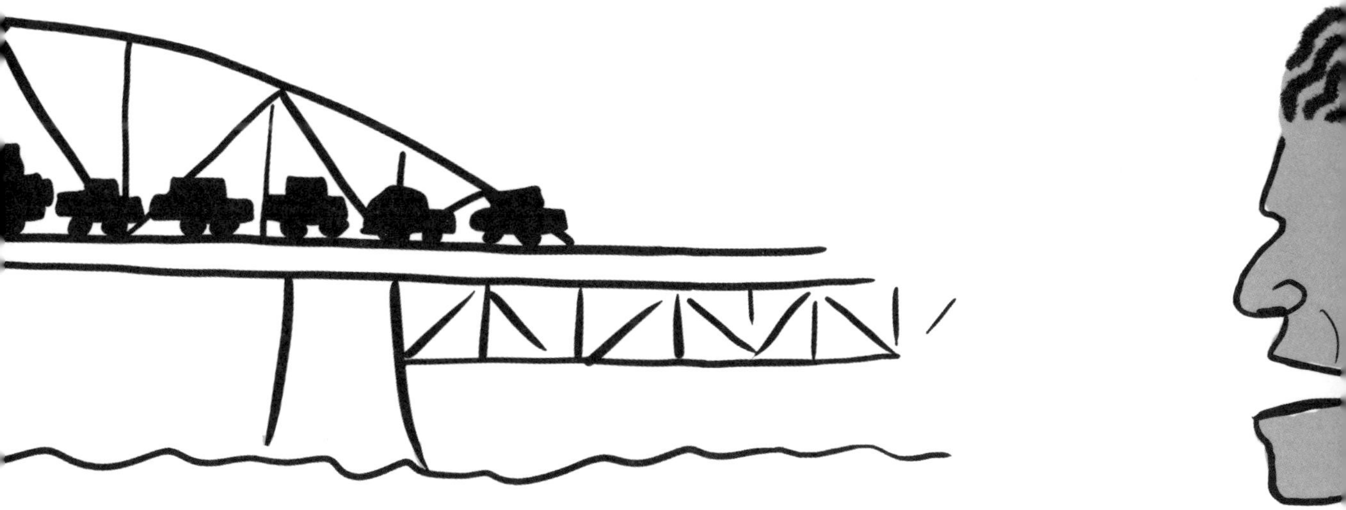

not block.

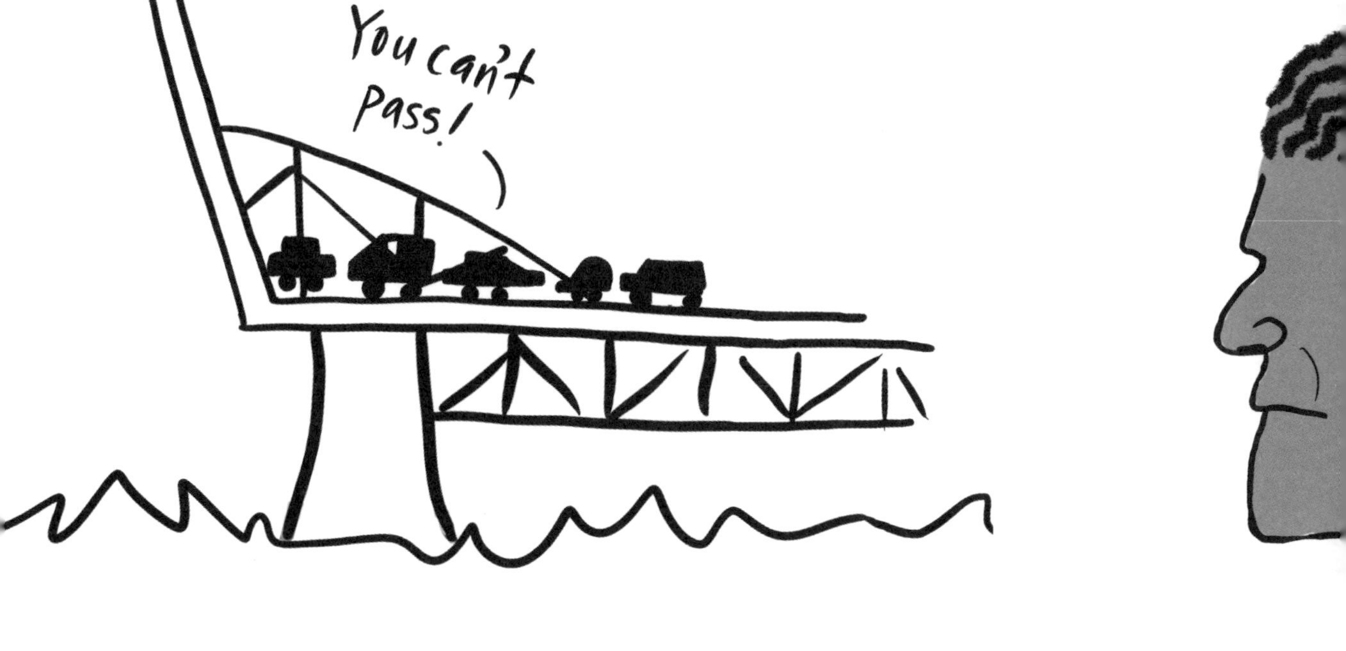
You can't pass!

So I ignored the sting.

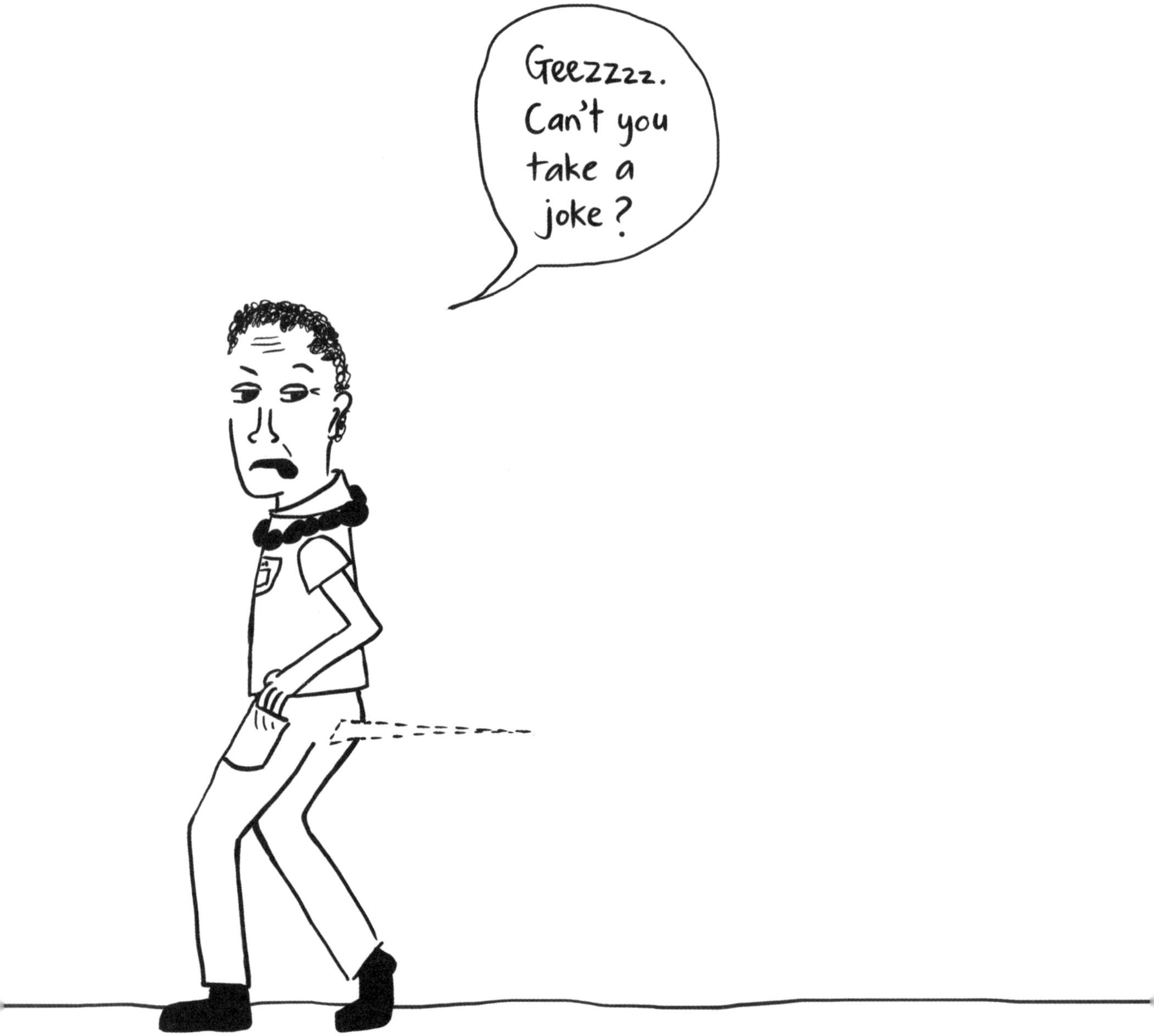
Geezzzz. Can't you take a joke?

Talk to the hand, bro...
Hello? Is this the Palace?

Yes, this is Barnabee, the Queen's helper.
Kia ora, it's Mophead, the Commonwealth poet.
Beeeautiful! Now, about the poem. You will perform it for the Queen in London.

In England?
It's the only London I know.
Actually, there's one in the Pacific.

Every year the Queen hosts Commonwealth Day at Westminster Abbey. All former colonies are invited.
Why?
Well, it marks our ALLIANCES.*
And ...
That's when you make up rules together.

...It marks our ALLEGIANCES.*
And...
?
... Um, our COLONIAL histories?
That's when you stick together because of the rules.
OUR LAND!
The Queen's!
Aaah!

That reminds me. The Queen has a few RULES.
No kidding.
5 to be exact.
Sure. Poets like rules...
...We like to break 'em!

RULE 1

The Queen chooses the event theme every year. This year it is UNITY.
Great!
That will be the title of your poem.
For real?
Is that a question?
Um... not really.

RULE 2
3,000 people are invited: 2,000 school children aged 9 and upwards, prime ministers, heads of state and of course, the ROYAL Family.
The poem will need to appeal to all of them.
Great!
For real?
Is that a question?

...Isn't the Duke of Edinburgh 94 years old?
GLOBAL CLIMATE CHAOS!
Yes, that's correct.
So the poem has to be fun for 9 year olds and 94 year olds?
Is that a question?
Yes.
That's one way to look at it.

RULE 3
There are 53 Commonwealth countries. The poem must include all of them.
Hmmm... challenging. What about an acrostic* poem?
A poem where the first letter of each line spells something.

A = Australia
B = Bangladesh
C = Cameroon
D = Dominica
E = Eswatini
F = Fiji
G = Ghana
I = India
All bridges connect,
divide, each frees
ground instantly ...

RULE 4
An acrostic poem might be a fine idea in theory,
BUT
the BBC
are filming live ...
... so the poem must not be longer than 3 minutes.

MOPPY MADNESS!

The rules were hard.

JOURNAL

I needed to build a bridge
from London's smoggy streets

to the sinking sands
in the South Seas.

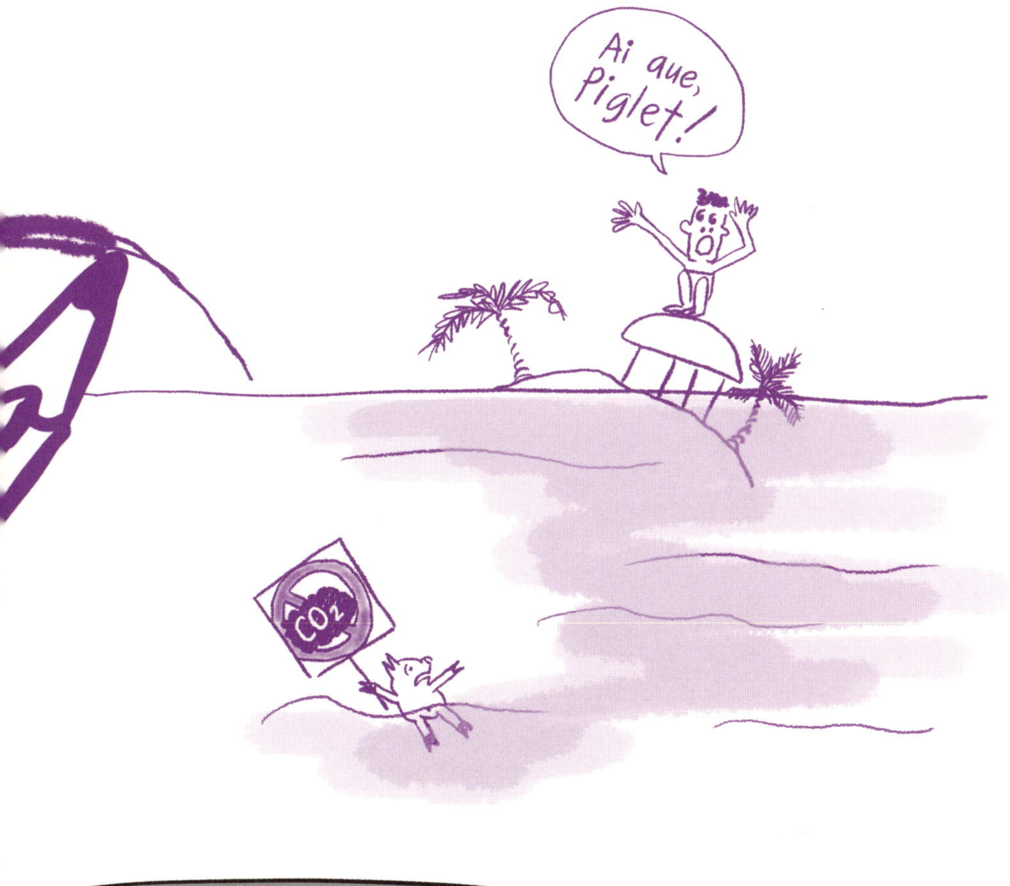
Ai aue, Piglet!
CO2

RULE 5
The 5th and final RULE is that the poem must not be POLITICAL*.
*That's how a country decides stuff!
Are floating piglets POLITICAL?
REDUCE CO_2

The poem will be checked by the Palace to make sure all the RULES are followed.
MOPPY MAYHEM!

There was a lot to think about.

RULE # 1
RULE # 2
RULE # 3 = THE QUEEN'S POEM
RULE # 4
RULE # 5

I had nine months to write the poem.

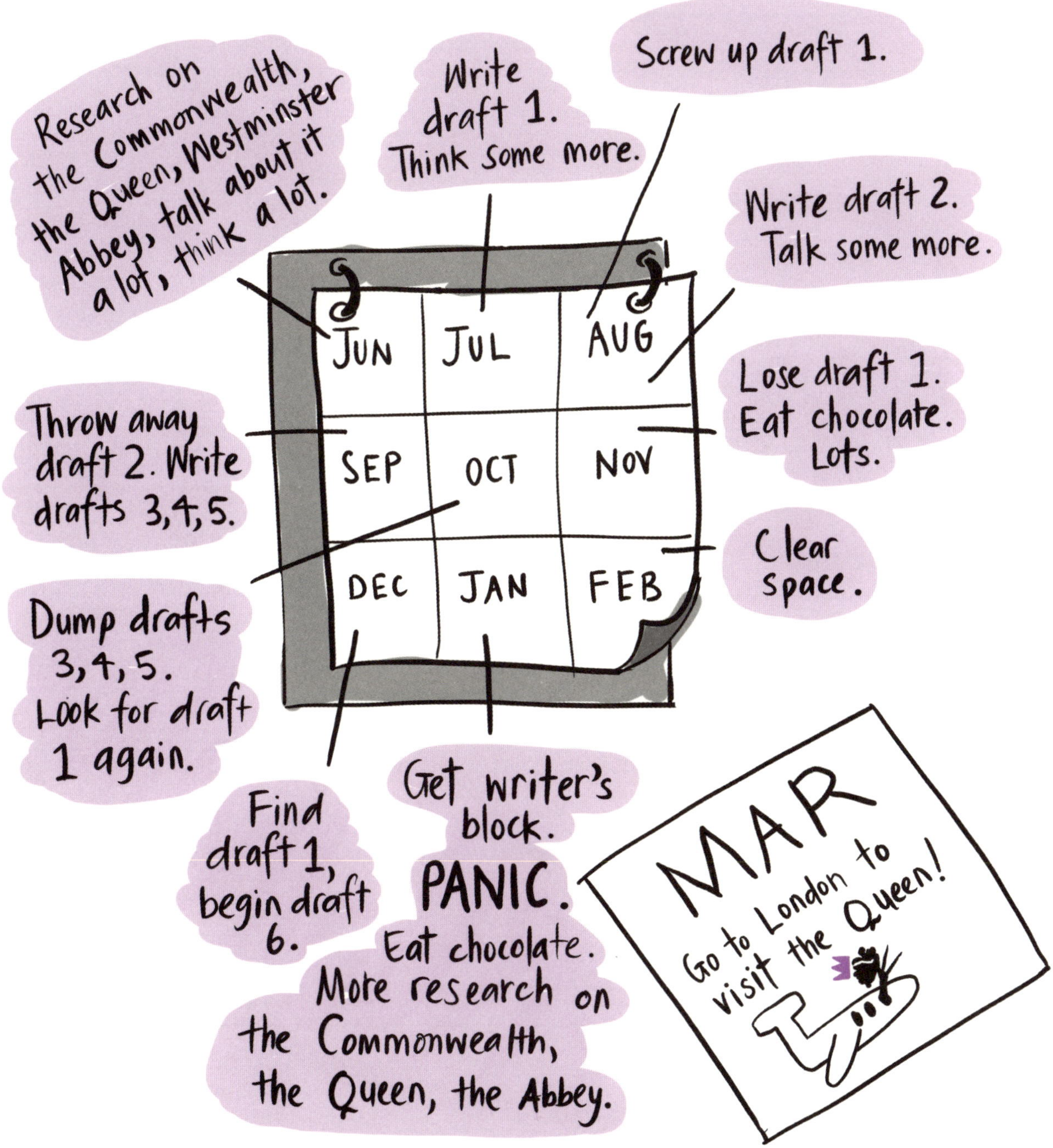
Research on the Commonwealth, the Queen, Westminster Abbey, talk about it a lot, think a lot.
Write draft 1. Think some more.
Screw up draft 1.
Write draft 2. Talk some more.
JUN
JUL
AUG
SEP
OCT
NOV
DEC
JAN
FEB
Throw away draft 2. Write drafts 3, 4, 5.
Lose draft 1. Eat chocolate. Lots.
Clear space.
Dump drafts 3, 4, 5. Look for draft 1 again.
Find draft 1, begin draft 6.
Get writer's block. PANIC. Eat chocolate. More research on the Commonwealth, the Queen, the Abbey.
MAR
Go to London to visit the Queen!

Each month passed.

NO POEM.

I pulled my hair out in

FRUSTRATION.

Then one Sunday I took a deep breath.

UNITY

EVERYBODY out of the house RIGHT NOW!

I'm driving!
Do we have cake?

Sweet – no drying the dishes!

I walked around and around the poem,

letting the title b-r-e-a-t-h-e.

Then
I
stood
in
the
middle
of
it
and
saw
the
ala.

There's a 'U' and an 'I' in UNITY!

I wrote the whole poem in a week
and sent it off to the Palace.

Then it came back.

Only one word was changed.

UNITY

It looked like I had followed the rules.

RULE #1 Title : Unity ✓
RULE #2 9-94 year olds ✓
RULE #3 53 Commonwealth nations ✓
RULE #4 <3 mins ✓
RULE #5 No politics ✓

But the Palace
doesn't
know
what poets
know.
my fine print

That a poem is a **TRICKSTER.**

You can't control it.

Māui, you tricked me out of my last fiery fingernail!
But Granny! I wanted to know where fire came from!
Oh, you're gonna know alright!!
MAHUIKA

That a poem is a

MIRAGE.

You can't believe
what you see.

What a fierce warrior he is!
Oi! That's a SHE...
...It's Nafanua, Goddess of War!

Where are we going, Nei Nim'anoa?
VOYAGING GODDESS
KIRIBATI
Somewhere marvellous, Mophead!

A poem is curious and brave,
taking you to unexpected places.

After the performance,
the Queen admired the poem.

How did you memorise that long poem?
It's my job, Your Majesty. I'm a poet.
Yes, I suppose it is. Well done.

The Duke forgot the poem.

So, what do you do?
I'm a poet, Your Royal Highness. I just performed... back there.

And two years later, Harry remembered the poem.

Why hello! It's the big-haired poet from the Abbey!
And this time I've got my tokotoko, my Poet Laureate walking stick.
Wanna see?

Harry took the tokotoko and stomped it on the ground.

YOU SHALL NOT PASS!

He was only having fun,
but his words hung around.

They reminded me of the Queen and her rules.

You shall pass.
You shall not pass.

But
rules
are
made
for

B R E A

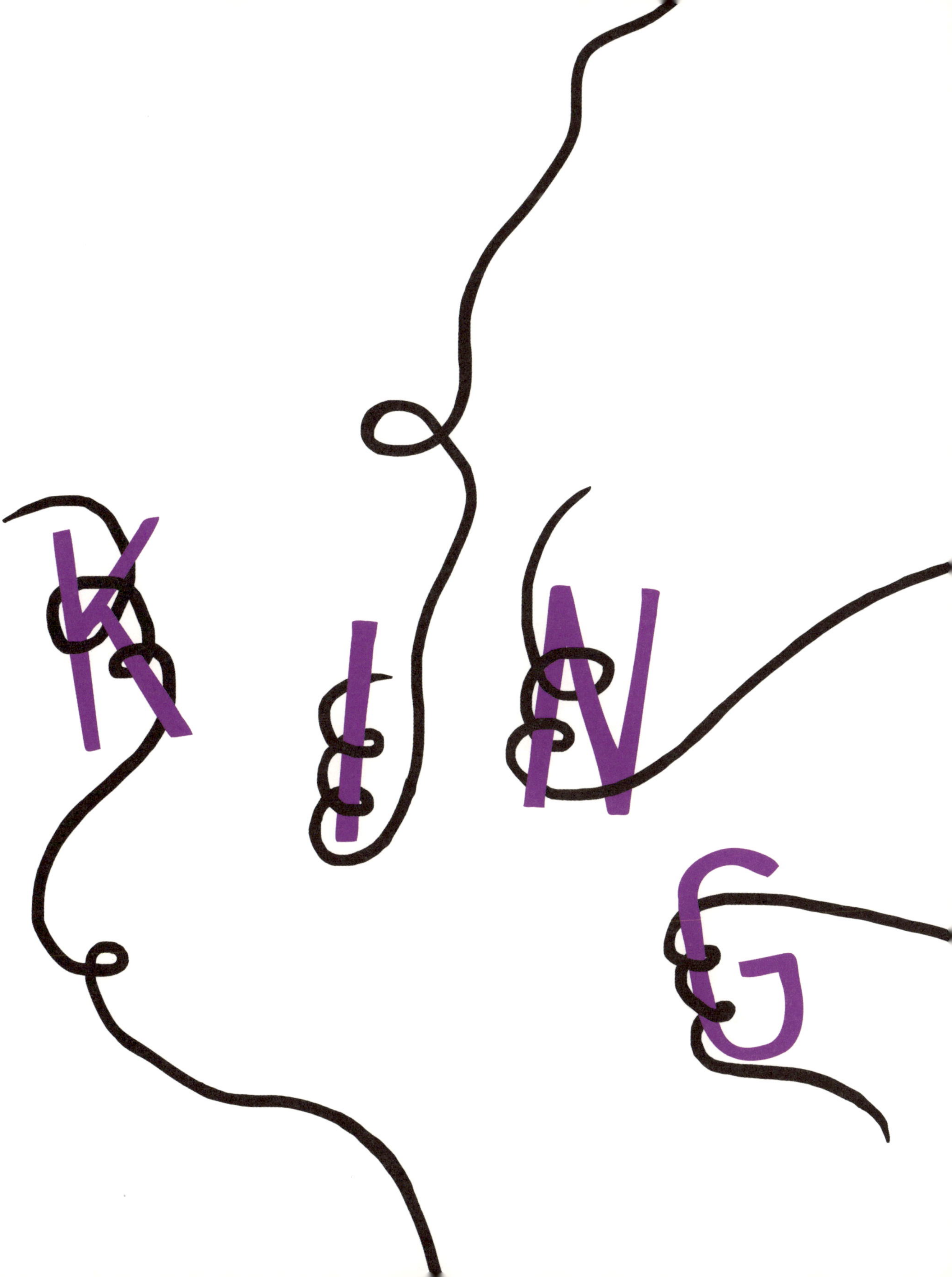
KING

Now, the Queen's family look different.

South Africa, I greet you not only as part of the Royal Family but as a woman of colour.
Sanibonani HRH Harry & Meghan

Our heroes look different.

Hang on, Māui! Wind is picking up!
But Nei Nim'anoa, I'm hungry!
Nafanua, you can chillax. I've read the stars.
Stick to navigation, Tupaia. I will defend us.

Our professors look different.

Even our poets look different.

Did you know there's a London in Kiribati...?
Where's Kiribati?
It used to be the Gilbert & Ellice Islands, dear.
Is that political?
Grandad, do get with it. It's a post-colonial* world.
Majesty
HRH
Harry

Professor Albert says the 'post' part doesn't just mean 'after' colonialism.
It also means around, against and alongside.
Alongside is where I stand.

So here we are.

The Queen from the Palace.

Just you and me.

Sharing our thoughts
over a cuppa tea

There's a 'U' and an 'I' in UNITY
Costs the earth
Yet it's FREE

'Cos where you stand matters!
the end

Fa'afetai & Thanks

Granny (Ilene Geboers née Miles) for her teacup
Luka & Sam for fights & make-ups

Janet for standing spaces
Helen for creative embraces

Beate for being over there
Tusiata for always being right here

Tina and her 2 for Tū
AUP Team (Sam, Sophia, Andy, Katharina) who do, do, do

Vida for storytelling page space
Sarah for faithfully setting the pace

Banyan for re-rooting the ala
Tana Tauhi Vā, my 4-legged fella

Vaughn & Rachel for their writing refuge
Dave for always being my dude

Javan, Micah & Davey, & all they make
The boy, the mole, the fox, the horse,

& all the cake!

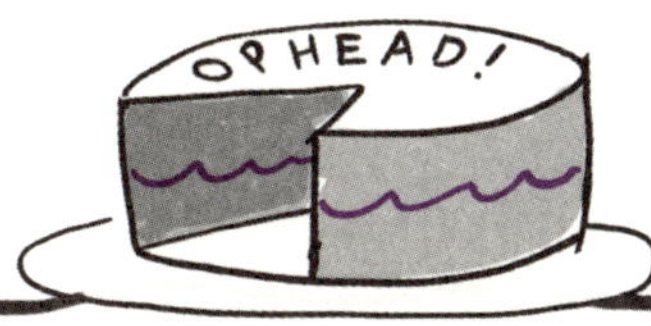

First published 2020
Auckland University Press
University of Auckland
Private Bag 92019
Auckland 1142
New Zealand
aucklanduniversitypress.co.nz

ISBN 978 1 86940 944 9

Published with the assistance of Creative New Zealand

creative nz
ARTS COUNCIL OF NEW ZEALAND TOI AOTEAROA

A catalogue record for this book is available
from the National Library of New Zealand

Design by Vida and Luke Kelly Design

Printed by 1010 Printing International Ltd

Albert Wendt's definition of 'post-colonial' can be found in *Nuanua: Pacific Writing in English since 1980* (Auckland: Auckland University Press, 1995).

The poem 'Unity' was published in *Tightrope* (Auckland: Auckland University Press, 2017).

Selina's complete journal for the Queen's poem can be found at
http://www.nzepc.auckland.ac.nz/features/tapa/marsh.asp

Fast Talking P.I.
Goes to London to visit the Queen
an ala is a
way finding
way faring
Commonwealth Observance Day
circa 1947
Commonwealth 14 March 2016
NZ House
The Commonwealth
Commonwealth Day Reception 2016
Dr Selina Tusitala Marsh
Reader at the Commonwealth Service
340
This opened Victoria Embankment
Abbey gates
Police barricades
Commonwealth minds
the Queen's eyes
fellow PI academic 'jokingly'
criticised me for accepting the Commonwealth
calling me a 'sell out', as if I don't know
The Pacific's colonial history, our problematic relationship with the Crown,
the social-political-historical context between Britain and the Pacific. This is alluded to in "Unity" — I mean, du-oh, why is there a London/Paris in Kiribati in the 1st place.
Kirimati
As always, the smart, witty retorts came later much later.
"My silences have not protected me. Your silence will not protect you."
- Audre Lorde
SPEAK OUT
SPEAK UP